Doreen Smith

T0088277

Violin Sight-Reading

Book 2

Music Department
OXFORD UNIVERSITY PRESS
Oxford and New York

NOTE

These graded sight-reading pieces for the violin are designed to provide practice material at all stages. Book 1 begins with the first position and covers the usual examination expectations for the earlier grades. More advanced players will find exercises requiring use of the higher registers, and the need for more technical expertise in book 2.

Fingering and bowing

There are as many fingerings and bowings as there are players. Those marked here are simply one way of performing a piece; they are by no means obligatory. The aim is to give as musical an impression as possible after a brief study of the piece, and to enjoy exploring the instrument.

To the violinist — what to do before you play

Look at:

- The **foreign words** which will suggest the speed, mood, and style.
- The **key signature**: work out your finger patterns on each string.
- The **time signature**: are you going to count in beats, or would it be more helpful to subdivide each beat?
- **Changes** of key signature or time signature (in higher grades).
- **Unusual** time patterns, accidentals, rests, staccato notes, slurs, and dynamics.
- The **speed**: decide on the speed and count at least one bar before you begin. Count aloud throughout.

Keep going, and try to give an overall impression of the music.

Doreen Smith, 1992

VIOLIN SIGHT-READING, BOOK 2

by DOREEN SMITH

GRADE 6

© Oxford University Press 1992

Reprinted by arrangement with Oxford University Press by Oxford University Press, Inc.

OXFORD UNIVERSITY PRESS, MUSIC DEPARTMENT, GREAT CLARENDON STREET, OXFORD OX2 6DP

Photocopying this copyright material is ILLEGAL.

Andante con tenerezza
4
p
*2nd position optional
poco cresc.
cresc.
poco rall.
poco cresc.
Vivo
5
mf
mp
mf
non legato
cresc.
Tempo di minuetto
6
p leggiero
mf
cresc.
mf
dim. e rall.

Presto
7
mf
p
mf
mp
cresc.
mf
p
cresc.
Amabile
8
p
mp
mf
p
dim.
Allegro marcato
9
f
rit.
poco rit.
a tempo

Lento
10
mp espressivo
dim. e poco rall.
Andante con moto
11
p
cresc.
p
poco a poco cresc.
mf
poco rall.
p
Alla gavotta
12
mp grazioso
p cresc.
poco dim.
mf
p
cresc.

Andante cantabile
13
p
mp
mf
p
cresc.
dim. e poco rit.
Risoluto
14
f
f
p
f
p
cresc.
f
Alla mazurka
15
p
poco più mosso
poco rall.
a tempo
p
cresc.
f

Andantino cantabile
16
mf
mp
p
rit.
a tempo
f
Sostenuto
17
p
mp
p
cresc.
Allegretto
18
p cantabile
poco cresc.
p
cresc.
rit.
p

Pastorale
19
p
mp
Giocoso
20
mf
poco rit.
a tempo

GRADE 7

Moderato
1
mp
mp
cresc.
dim.
p

2
Alla marcia
f
poco rit.
a tempo
pizz.
3
Tranquillo
mp
dim.
p
4
Andantino
mp dolce
scherzando

Andante espressivo
5
mf
mp
mf
dim.
cantabile
poco rit.
a tempo
mf
rit. e dim.
Allegretto grazioso
6
mf
p
cresc.
dim. e rit.
Andante moderato
7
p
mf
f
dim.

Allegretto
8
mp
cresc.
p
mf
mp
dim. e poco rit.
Alla mazurka
9
f marcato
p dolce
f marcato
p dolce
Allegro
10
mf
p
cresc.

Moto perpetuo
Presto
11
f
Allegretto piacevole
12
mf leggiero
Animato
f pesante
p dolce
f
f pesante
p dolce
tempo primo
mf leggiero
f
Allegro moderato
13
p legato
cresc.
cresc.
p
cresc.
dim. e rit.

Largo
14
mf sostenuto
p
cresc.
cresc.
Allegro marcato
15
f
più mosso
p scherzando
poco meno mosso
poco rit.
a tempo
f
Andantino
16
mp
mf
p
mp poco rit. e dim.

Vivace
17
f
mf
sostenuto

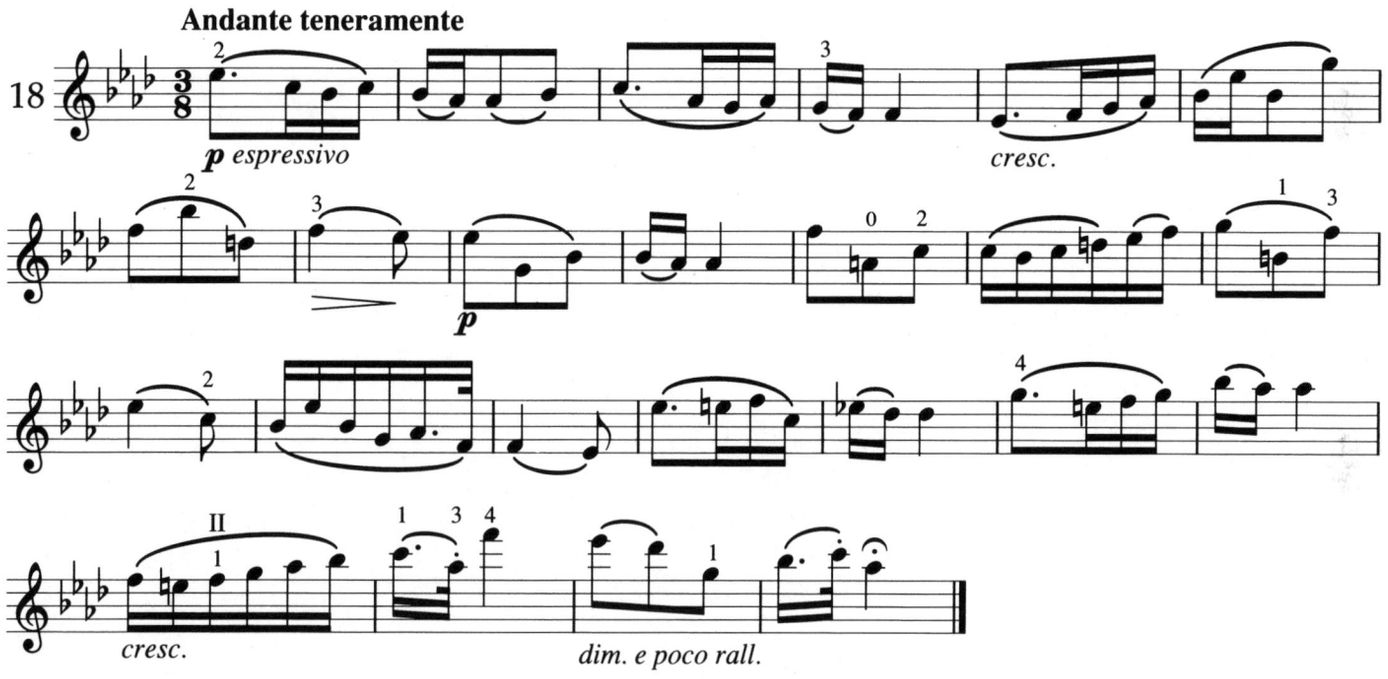
Andante teneramente
18
p espressivo
cresc.
p
cresc.
dim. e poco rall.

Giocoso
19
mf
meno f
f

Lento cantabile
20
p
mp
dim. e poco rit.

GRADE 8

Slow 'blues' tempo
1
mp
p
cresc.
f
dim. e rall.

Allegretto grazioso
2
mp
mp
mf
p
cresc.
Burlesque
3
mp
cresc.
f
poco rit.
a tempo
mp
cresc.
f
Andante grazioso
4
pleggiero
cresc.
p
p
pp

Andantino
5
mf
cresc.
mf
poco dim.
mp
mf
Mesto
6
mp
cresc.
mf
rit.
a tempo
p
cresc.
mf
dim. e poco rall.
Vivo scherzando
7
mf
mf
dim.
p
cresc.
f

Tristemente
8
p legato
p
mp
dim.

Tempo di minuetto
9
mf
p
p

Allegretto
10
mf
p dolce
dim. e poco rit.
a tempo
mf

Lento
11
p
mp
cresc.
Tempo di gavotta
12
mp
cresc.
poco rit.
a tempo
cresc.
Larghetto
13
p
cresc.
p
mf
dim. e rit.

Allegro scherzando
14
mf
mp
mf
cresc.
Lento moderato
15
p
cresc.
dim. e rit.
Allegretto giusto
16
mf
p
cresc.

Vivo
17
mp
p
mp
p
mp
cresc.

Moderato
18
mp
cresc.
cresc.

Allegro con spirito
19
mf
cresc.
mp
cresc.
mf
f
Allegro con brio
20
f
pizz.
arco
pizz.
arco
mf
mp
mf
mp
f
pizz.
arco
f